NAME YOUR EMOTIONS

SOMETIMES I FEEL HAPPY

by Jaclyn Jaycox

PEBBLE

a capstone imprint

Pebble Emerge is published by Pebble, an imprint of Capstone.
1710 Roe Crest Drive
North Mankato, Minnesota 56003
www.capstonepub.com

Library of Congress Cataloging-in-Publication Data is available on the
Library of Congress website.
ISBN 978-1-9771-2462-3 (library binding)
ISBN 978-1-9771-2638-2 (paperback)
ISBN 978-1-9771-2505-7 (eBook PDF)

Summary: What does it mean to be happy? Children will learn what
happiness feels like, how their senses can affect their emotions, and
how to name and manage their feelings. Full-color, diverse photos help
illustrate what happiness looks like. A mindfulness activity gives kids
the opportunity to explore their feelings.

Image Credits
Capstone Studio: Karon Dubke, 21; Shutterstock: Africa Studio, 17,
Alissala, 5, Color Symphony, Design Element, KPG Payless2, 9, Maria
Evseyeva, 13, MIA Studio, Cover, Monkey Business Images, 15, Rido,
18, SeventyFour, 6, Valeria Selezneva, 7, Watercolor_Art_Photo, 11,
wavebreakmedia, 19

Editorial Credits
Designer: Kay Fraser; Media Researcher: Tracy Cummins; Production
Specialist: Katy LaVigne

All internet sites appearing in back matter were available and accurate
when this book was sent to press.

Printed and bound in China.
3322

TABLE OF CONTENTS

Words in **bold** are in the glossary.

WHAT IS HAPPINESS?

Happiness is an **emotion**, or feeling. It is OK to have lots of different feelings every day. Some last for just a few minutes. But others may last longer.

Some emotions make you feel good. Others make you feel bad. Happiness is a good feeling!

WHAT DOES IT FEEL LIKE TO BE HAPPY?

Close your eyes. Think of something that makes you happy. Maybe it's playing with friends. Or watching a funny movie. How do you feel?

Feelings start in the brain. They move through your body. When you are happy, you smile and giggle. Your heart beats fast. You may even jump up and down!

USING YOUR SENSES

People have five **senses**. We can hear, smell, and touch things. We can also taste and see things. Your senses can spark different feelings.

Hearing a good song can make you feel happy. Smelling flowers might make you happy. Touching a soft puppy can make you happy.

TALKING ABOUT YOUR FEELINGS

Talking about your feelings helps you deal with them. At first it can be hard to talk about how you feel. But that is OK! It just takes a little practice.

When you feel happy, say the emotion out loud. Talk to someone about why you feel happy. It is good practice. It will make it easier to talk about sad or mad feelings.

11

UNDERSTANDING HAPPINESS

It is important to understand feelings. What makes you feel happy? Maybe you got an award at school. Maybe you made a new friend.

How you feel about yourself can affect your emotions. It is easier to be happy when you feel good about yourself.

13

Happiness can be helpful. When you are happy, you feel **positive** and cheerful. It helps you get along with others. You may have more energy. You do your best work when you are happy. You are more creative and a better learner.

HANDLING YOUR FEELINGS

There are no good or bad emotions. How you handle them is what matters. Maybe you are feeling down. There are many ways to make yourself happy.

Going for a walk can make you feel happier. Listening to music helps too. Even just smiling will put you in a good **mood**!

You can help others be happy too.
Happiness should be shared. Say
something nice to someone who looks sad.
Do a good **deed** for a person in need.

Sometimes people try to keep their feelings inside. But it is important to share them with people you care about. It can help you feel closer to them.

MINDFULNESS ACTIVITY

A weather report tells us what the weather is like. Some days it is gloomy. Other days it is sunny. Emotions are like the weather.

What You Do:

1. Write a weather report on how you are feeling. Are there raindrops falling from your eyes? Are there rays of sunshine all around you?

2. Draw a picture based on your weather report.

Good morning.

My name is Josie.

I am excited to share today's

weather forecast with you!

Today is going to be a

great day full of sunshine.

Be sure to get outside to

spread kindness on this happy

sunny day. Don't forget your

sunglasses!

GLOSSARY

deed (DEED)—something that is done

emotion (i-MOH-shuhn)—a strong feeling; people have and show emotions such as happiness, sadness, fear, anger, and jealousy

mood (MOOD)—the way that you are feeling

positive (PAH-zi-tiv)—helpful or upbeat

sense (SENSS)—a way of knowing about your surroundings; hearing, smelling, touching, tasting, and sight are the five senses

READ MORE

Kreul, Holde. *My Feelings and Me*. New York: Skyhorse Publishing, 2018.

Nilsen, Genevieve. *Happy*. Minneapolis: Jump!, Inc., 2018.

INTERNET SITES

Emotions Coloring Pages
www.coloring.ws/emotion.htm

Kids' Health – Feelings
https://kidshealth.org/en/kids/feeling/?WT.ac=k-nav-feeling

INDEX